common place ecstasies

common place ecstasies

poems by

wendy mcgrath

Porcepic Books
an imprint of

Beach Holme Publishing
Vancouver

This book is published by Beach Holme Publishing, 226–2040 West 12th Avenue, Vancouver, B.C. V6J 2G2. This is a Porcepic Book.

The publisher gratefully acknowledges the financial support of the Canada Council for the Arts and of the British Columbia Arts Council. The publisher also acknowledges the financial assistance received from the Government of Canada through the Book Publishing Industry Development Program (BPIDP) for its publishing activities.

The Canada Council | Le Conseil des Arts
for the Arts | du Canada

BRITISH
COLUMBIA
ARTS COUNCIL
Supported by the Province of British Columbia

Editor: Michael Carroll
Production and Design: Jen Hamilton
Cover Art: *The Twisted Veil, site of imagined opposition* by Walter Jule, 1998. 100 x 70 centimetres, etching, lithograph, chine collé. Collection of the artist. Used with permission.
Author Photograph: John McGrath

Printed and bound in Canada by Marc Veilleux Imprimeur

Canadian Cataloguing in Publication Data

McGrath, Wendy.
  Common place ecstasies

  "A Porcepic book."
  Poems.
  ISBN 0-88878-411-2

  I. Title.
PS8575.G74C65 2000   C811'.6   C00-910660-X
PR9199.3.M3165C65 2000

For John

contents

acknowledgements   ix

in that same house   *1*

after van Gogh's *The Night Café*   3

wedding portrait   5

Leask, Sask.   7

early musical experiences   8

carpenter's rules   9

brown boots   10

pink house   11

in that same house   12

another house   different summer   13

augury   14

sand   15

language barrier   16

weeds   17

sweet pink   18

space   19

CN Tower 20

Tupperware party 21

preserving *23*

preserving 25

margarine 41

eggs 42

bananas 44

trees 45

berry picking 46

rhubarb 47

properties of cement 48

outside 49

fingers of women/marking time *51*

desire 53

rope 54

train trestle 55

touch sites 56

fingers of women/marking time 57

waitress suite 59

elements of expectation 67

noise 69

wash day 70

my mother's relationship with fire 71

Jean 73

knitting 74

company 76

ghosts 77

she 79

secret language 80

words about birth 81

acknowledgements

Thanks to family and friends for their support—John, Eamon, Brendan, Ann Burgos, Shelly Hines, Maureen McGrath, Linda Gauthier, Shelagh Kubish, and Elaine Hoogewoonink.

Thanks to my grandmothers for creating a path.

Thanks to Michael Carroll and the staff at Beach Holme.

Thanks to Joy Gugeler.

Thanks to Bert Almon and Doug Barbour for their encouragement.

Thanks to my father for teaching me acceptance and forgiveness.

Thanks to Walter Jule for allowing me to use his remarkable print for the cover of this book.

Thanks to the following magazines in which versions of these poems appeared: *absinthe, blue buffalo, CV2, Dandelion, Grain, ORBIS, Prism international, Room of One's Own, Secrets from the Orange Couch, Tessera*, the League of Canadian Poets' *Vintage 97–98*, and various Edmonton *Stroll of Poets* anthologies.

Thanks also to CBC Radio for producing and broadcasting a version of "preserving."

in that same house

after van Gogh's The Night Café

red

silver/ash tips
of cigarettes smoked
red rivets of talk
shot inside
this closed space
unequal triangle
the painted shape inside
my mother's arm bent
on the back of the seat

green

lights from the dash
my father
staring
at the night café
husky truck stop
1/2 way point
radio scurs and spits
at signals left behind
clock   stopped   long   ago

red

vinyl seats
chrome napkin holders
plastic clock plugged in
behind the milkshake maker
jukebox on the table
songs flipping past
clicking past

the night café
the shortcut
of the waitress's hair
bony face
the distance travelled
our forced brightness
as she brings the food
my father tells us
he got his education
in the pool hall

wedding portrait
after van Eyck

1.

>>> the bride drinks deep   from her cigarette
>>>>> black coffee from a yellow Melmac cup
>>> refusing to grasp the subtle hierarchy of lot and location
>>>>> choice of fabric
>>>>> kind of dog
>>>>> style of flower bed

>>> the groom quiet after a day hearing
>>>>> hammers   electric saws chewing wood
>>> car radio blasting tin sound out an open door

> my parents picked out their "piece of the pie" from a brochure
>>>>> Honeymoon Village
> new subdivision   corner lot   950-square-foot house
>>>>> no wasted space

2.

one shelf in the kitchen
was lined in glasses engraved with ALCB
we measured milk to the white line
drank and looked through its clouded convex mirror

Maxine and Mom smuggled them from
the Transit Hotel in big black vinyl purses
laughed at the look on the waitress's face
when she came to collect empties

the next morning a sinkful of tall glasses
our kitchen smelling of beer   dried foam
a filigree around each rim

3.

mirror tiles at our front door
my father shouting at my reflection
tie-dyed T-shirt   ripped jeans   dirty runners
        you look like a DP
        here   take some money
        never leave the house without money
        if they find you ten miles from home
        with less than a dime in your pocket
        they'll pick you up for vagrancy
        in spring all the nuts come out
        they'll just hit you over the head
        throw you in the back of a truck
        and that'll be the end of you

4.

my father talked to the bathroom mirror too
        sonnuvvabitch I was busy today
        I look like the *Wreck of the Hesperus*
then held his breath as he washed
concrete dust and dirt and sawdust stuck to his skin
a whole day   building

5.

after supper   silence

two of them smoking
        Exports
        and Cameos
flicking sections of the newspaper
drinking weak tea
from stained cups

Leask, Sask.

wool-wrapped and speechless
in the cold back seat

Grandfather drove us downtown
to see the Christmas lights
three strings across
Main Street   where cars parked crook-neck
in front of   Hanson's Café   The Big Store   OK Economy

       don't go into the beer parlour
       and leave them waiting
       my mother warned

he didn't   but drove slowly past
those steamy baroque-lit hotel windows
sometimes he forgot our names

early musical experiences

my parents joined a record club
12 records for 99 cents

my mother checked the *easy listening* box
ordered Wayne Newton and Mario Lanza

I ordered Beatles *Rubber Soul*   Pet Clark *This Is My Song*
my father ordered The Lettermen

others came later
arriving unannounced   unchosen
Dean Martin   Bing Crosby

when Frank Sinatra showed up
my father fired him back with a letter

send me another goddamn record
and I'll send it back
in so many pieces

carpenter's rules

love has nothing to do with order
it is anarchy   unplaned doors and odd-sized windows
random shoots of
                        electrical wire   rebar   snap ties

yellow carpenter's pencil   flat and sharpened with a knife
stacks of change on a chest of drawers
                        a watch's face gone cloudy from sweat

there are no rules
for the amount of time a light is turned on or off
how long we leave the fridge door open
            coffeepot boiling   on the stove
how many sunflower seeds we spit on the car floor

all just estimation
yards of concrete   sheets of plywood
                        piles of two-by-fours

brown boots

lined with layers
of newspaper
to keep out the cold

fit the frame of bones
as you walked planks
     50 cents an hour
fit the frame of bones
as you put in footings
     50 cents an hour
of basements you poured
watching cement set
     50 cents an hour

end of day
loosened laces
hanging tongues
moulded these boots
into the shape
of leaving

pink house

I knelt on the grass
felt the sound of   green
and it was cool
beside our small pink house
one window open
faint noises
inside   safe

I was happy to say nothing
         not to have to choose
words

                    right ones   wrong ones
                    just be   quiet

I pulled the arms of my doll through
holes of a dress my mother made
green fabric with six-sided circles
and inside an *O*
I said that letter over and over
the cool of grass of green shade
in the circle of that letter
safe in the sound of cupboard doors shutting
silver-plated armour of knives and forks   silence
a thin black line enclosing
this house   a girl   a doll

in that same house

I am lying in bed
floor shining back at the sun
afternoon and I am expected to sleep
but all I can see is the sun   bright
with its own expectations
my father is sitting on a chair
too small   beside my bed
tells me he will stay until I sleep

and my hand is holding his   tight
beside my pillow
callused and thick-fingered

      and I say
      stay   stay until I go to sleep
      and the sun is shifting its position on the floor
      my father stays   holds my hand
      looking out the window
      and I say
                  just stay

another house   different summer

     made a tent
         from a good white sheet
             clipped two corners   middle
        to our whitewithcoraltrim fence

split clothespins became pegs
driven into the ground
with my father's hammer

     inside that tent
     hair wet   I read about Anne
     wanting my hair   green
     ran fingers over two braids Mom made
     felt the furrowed part white   cool middle

     pulled the elastics off the thin points
     tips of paintbrushes
     unravelled lengths of hair   made perfectly equal
     cool waves   damp from the pool

     a wide piece of grass   held tight between my thumbs
     air
     and a thin green tongue

augury

you found that bird
that black bird
dead
by the front step
treated it like a doll
picked up/played with
wrapped in white cloth

       she's playing with a dead thing
       I said

it was snatched away
something dirty
to be buried
in the backyard

       we were assured
       it would go to heaven

sand

were you smiling
when we ran through the bushes

stopped
to watch a hummingbird frozen in midair?
did your hands   small and soft
(with your fingernails bit to stubs)
clap   clap   clap
before the bird flew?

you were a stain on the rotting wood floor that said *S*
a name the sound of sand
behind me on the narrow stairs
you touched the small of my back
afraid of creaking boards
and dirty broken windows

you saw a dead mouse
under the disappearing front porch
and held it in your hands

language barrier

my sister and I invented a language
thin bands of sound making sense
only to us

on bowling banquet night
we talked over tic-tac-toe
X-ed with bobby pins on our mother's head
our parents spoke as if we were invisible

> *you don't have to talk to everybody right?*
> *now you're just talkin' stupid*
> *I might not say nothin'   but I'll be watchin'*

we abandoned our creation
stopped understanding
realized the word *happiness*
was untranslatable   overused and
underfelt

weeds

that was the summer my sister grew six inches
her legs aching with growing

stretch marks waxed
narrow pink crescents
across the small of her back

her own muscles woke her
       charley horse charley horse
Dad grabbing her ankles
pounding her feet on the floor
      we'll send them back where they came from

everything calmed
he guided her back to bed
so she could grow
another two inches by morning

sweet pink

silver razor   reclining cold on glass
Noxzema's blue jar
an enamel coat spread over my face
tingled magic   the way I imagined myrrh

small vial of pale tablets
children's aspirin   sweet and pink

as my mother slept
I climbed onto the sink
ate as many as I could before confessing
telling my sister to have some too

at the hospital
the nurse asked how many
I held up both hands
spread my fingers   as wide as I could

space

my sister poked a knife at our dog's nose
I grabbed the blade
between thumb and index finger

our mother ran cold water into the sink
held my hand under
      tetanus   stitches   lockjaw
I kept my mouth frozen open in a shape
that might still give me voice

the blood was quite beautiful
clouds   red and aching out into space

CN Tower

I held a comb under the tap and tried to tuck the loose hairs
back into my braids   pulled my socks right up to my knees
my father was already needing a shave since I saw him that
morning   my parents smoked cigarettes in the front seat with
all the windows open and my brother sat on my mother's lap
playing with her set of keys

going downtown in our Galaxie 500 to see the tallest building
in Edmonton   was it as big as the Empire State Building and
where was that anyway   could we see it through the clouds
27 stories high and I could read what it was *C* filling liquid red
overflowing into *N* and all of it being sucked back out again
and where did that colour come from and where was it going

Tupperware party

when my mother got home my brother's diaper was full of shit
the sink was full of dishes my sister and I up past bedtime
throwing a redbluewhite rubber ball against the kitchen wall
my father lost in *Hogan's Heroes* an ashtray full of butts beside
him

we brought out the Ouija board and I'm sure nobody was pushing
it the board was really answering questions things about me no
one would know finally it just got tired said goodbye   that was that

I thought her beautiful in orange lipstick brown high heels   the
scent of Evening in Paris   she changed my brother's diaper put
him crying in his crib   tucked a dishtowel in the neck of her
one good dress did dishes with a run in her one good pair of
nylons already sneaking its way up her rough left heel sent us
to bed

if you put one foot on the floor you'll be sorry how did this pot
get burnt?

and my father saying he tried to make us popcorn forgot the
burner was on until he saw the reflection of the fire in the living-
room window   she wiped soot from the ceiling

lucky you didn't burn the place down

when the Tupperware lady delivered salt 'n pepper shakers   a
green salad bowl with a white lid my mother was happy took
them from their cellophane wrappers

this is no ordinary plastic

preserving

preserving

my mother was taught to seal jars
with paraffin or rubber rings

chokecherries congeal
in juices
pin cherries prick the jelly bag

preserved and embalmed
they stare from jars
old labels   soaked off

whispers   inside

Types of Jars

Test the seal—
A. **By sound:**
    1. **clear ring—seal all right.**
    2. **hollow ring—open jar, put new**
       top on, reprocess.

B. **By sight: if lids are slightly drawn**
    in, seal is satisfactory.

Gramma got this capping machine
don't know why she didn't want Grampa
drinking anyway she did 250 beer bottles
full of peas all we heard all night was
pop   pop   pop
trying to get out

**Test rubber ring. Fold between fingers
and discard if there are any cracks.**

rubberrings   rubber rings   rubber   rings
rubbers   French safes
hasty marriage   two rings
five babies   five big babies
two girls   three boys
born at home

Do not stretch synthetic rubber rings.

we used sealer rings
to hold up our stockings
stretched them out a bit
folded the tops of our stockings over them
no one the wiser

the rings on our skin
as red
as sealer rings

Begin to count the time
when water reaches
a "bumping" boil

the difference
between
a fast boil and a slow boil

tell me the difference
tell me   when
to   start   counting

**Even the beginner can avoid
unnecessary waste of sugar, fruits, and vegetables,
and can feel confident of successful results if she
will follow**

in her footsteps?
hardly possible with
five toes on the right foot
four toes on the left
the label of your
stubborn nature

how many times
did you complain
to the doctor
who cut it off   just
because of a corn

Fish

**Prepare fresh-caught, thoroughly bled fish
as for cooking. The backbone may be left in small fish—
remove it from larger ones.**

grade two art class: soap carving

                             a fish from Sunlight soap
              yellow and   I could read its name
      sun/light
                  clean

                                stark

soap yielding under the knife
I lifted scales from its flat surface
gouged eyes with knife tip
my heartbeat throat tight
sharp points dangerous
in a seven-year-old hand

21 years later
sun/light soap
microwaved in Pyrex
breathing in
burning fumes

        I couldn't speak for a week

By sound:
By sight:

       no sound of

                 the sun
       no sound of

              3 in the afternoon
         the one time   my mother remembered
         as a child

being afraid   everyone
was sleeping   it was

              3 in the afternoon and
everyone was
sleeping and   she remembered

remembered   being afraid
of having

         no shadow to outrun
         no voice to shout down the sky
         no sound of
               the sun
such a laughing liar
of unrelenting
         no shade   unhiding

If a very transparent jelly is desired,
strain hot juice through a cloth
heavy enough
to hold back particles
hold back
          forgiveness
                    hold back
                              love
hold back
          why do you always hold back   my lover says to me
there's something you're
                              holding back
holding back   holding   back

Aristocracy Pickle (Mustard)

my grandmother sits on a gold vinyl recliner
covered with a granny-square afghan
two miniature apricot poodles doze beside her

I sit on a worn brown couch that smells of dog
we watch Carol Pope and Rough Trade
on a television nestled inside a glossy cabinet
masquerading as fine furniture

You know   I could never eat
prunes or macaroni
my mother thought nothing
was ever good enough
no one
was ever good enough
for me

I wonder what
she would think of
instant potatoes or
instant coffee or
me?

> Grampa-Great spread buns with rat
> poison
> put them in the shed
> my cousin
>   (about three at the time)
> just about to take a bite
> of one of them when
> our dog jumped up and ate it right out
> of his hand
>
>   it took him two days to die

Bitter Orange Marmalade

**Bring pulp to a boil
until skins are tender.**

at Christmastime
one Japanese orange
in our stocking
squeeze it make it

soft
           put off   eating it
           as long
as   we   could

           bitter orange   skin scent
           winter inside   out

my aunt would smell oranges
when she was going to have   oranges
a fit   she'd say
when she was going to have
a fit   she would always smell   oranges

This is where my grandmother occurred in winter   this is the
place she was   in between the periods   of *Hockey Night
in Canada* she was in   Saskatchewan   in between
cigarette smoke trailing up toward the ceiling   yellow as a
church ceiling ringed   tallow-circled   in between crocheted
wool stitches   smell of her dogs wet siwash wool in the back
porch   smell of old wood   dust

Answers to Canning Problems

**When dill pickles break
jar seals and bubble,
are they spoiled?**

Shall I toss them out?

*Don't throw out the baby
with the bathwater*

Saturday was bath night
five kids bathing in
the same water
the last one
a cold
soap
soak
dunk
jump   in and out

Cucumber Supreme

**Put 7 large, well-washed cucumbers
through the mincer. Add 2 tbsp. salt.
Let stand all night and drain.**

every Saturday when Mom and Dad went to town
Myrna and I would clean up the house
make a big plate of scrambled eggs
this relish on the side
settle in with a *True Story*

I looked for that recipe for years

Strawberry Jam

strawberry   runners

strawberries   running

wild   we were running

wild between the graves plotting

our course   graveyard

no one goes to

         tend it   no one goes

and it rained it rained it rained

we were running

      between the graves   picking the

strawberries   running wild between the graves

Maraschino Cherries

Remove cherries, wash thoroughly, and pit.

stones from the stoneboat   she throws them on the pile
of stones   and turning from the stones
she is like Michelangelo's unfinished sculpture
from an unfinished tomb
The Dying Slave
struggling to break free from the stone
separate   but still part of it
clink   chip   heavy on the pile
turning away from the stones she reaches free
but never really free because
she is the stone itself
stone   pit
a name   her name started soft
ended hard
                              like her
Jean   with no middle name

filling jars   filling them with what was
in between   inside
filling them with words

margarine

that slab of white wax
painted yellow   a disc of powdered gold
its mystery hidden under parchment
pigment my mother mixed with bare hands

        I cupped my hands
        over steam from the kettle
        but my wrists
        burned brightest

the worst kind of burns   my mother said
they burn twice   once from heat
                        once from water

rubbing margarine   salve on my palms
upturned on the kitchen table
it'll sink in   she said

        I stuck my finger
        through the wire mask
        of a ticking metal fan
        wanting it under skin and bone

this time my mother painted with
Mercurochrome   red over red
and asked
why

eggs

1. fish

something to do with Audrey Hepburn
        caviar   sevruga   smallest fish eggs
        sweet in my imagination
        pearls   cigarette holder   full-length gloves

northern pike   jackfish
        caught in spring when they're full of eggs
        gutted and filleted   white
        fried in hot margarine served in brittle chunks

2. fried

my grandmother brought in enough
for everyone's breakfast
collected from the coop   cradled in her apron
marked with bits of straw specks of dirt
wiped and cracked over a hot frying pan

one with a blood spot
red   bright against the yolk
its white weaving a lace edge from the heat

3. Easter

eggs sculling in colour
red   blue   yellow   sheeting from silver
spoons we used to move warm   brown eggs
in clear glass bowls
dye stained our fingers   circled our nails
as we set the eggs to dry on newspaper
ads   for mufflers   farm equipment   passion

4. earth and sky

the Phoenicians believed
we were created from halves
of an   egg

                    their purple   extracted from glands of snails
                    leaving soft sea bodies to rot in hot sun

5. empty shells

crushed to stop witches
using them for boats
these vessels once contained all elements
finding a double-yolked egg   good luck
the universe dividing
a small cell of air
marking its first breath?

bananas

blackening yellow tapers
splayed and dotted
soften by exposure
to inarticulate air

fingers curve outward
unfurl silence
a bristling black spider
waits to bite

trees

1. witching

Y-shaped branch
      forking twisted
            follows hill curve
                  bedrock and spring
                          silent geography
                  underfoot
              trapped branch divines
          silent geometry underground
      rock and river
spring invisible

              2. whistling

                  knife cut
                  whistle chunk mouthpiece
                  delicate greenbark   still
                  poplar flute

                            tree song

berry picking

pine needles yielded
        blue
        berries smug   small

austere in mottled light
        she kept close to the ground
        with fingers stained
        reached innocently
        for that hollow under her arm

there
        and felt it
        her death
        small as a berry
                red

        in the mirror at home
        she wiped
            hard
        trying to erase
        the stain of her own touch

rhubarb

on the stove
stiff stalks turn   soft
and when stirred   slowly
their threads articulate paisley

      sullen glass jars to be filled
      sting of vinegar   allspice   ginger   cloves
      sweet   and hot
inside jars   already absorbed and invisible

the touch of his middle finger   cool
smoothing hard bone that begins her spine
walls dream sweat   shivering in the heat

properties of cement

memory is a shifting of stone and sand
when recollections harden they are not always smooth
taking the form of an imagined reverse
emptiness made solid   space made shape

so
when I come to you and say   *remember when*
let me leave a handprint on this grey surface

outside

this hospital room
is every place my father has ever slept
empty bottles   three packs of smokes a day
the life he found   wanting
until unable to raise a hammer   hold steady a saw
he lay down on that last job site

outside has folded into
wood-putty pink walls
a green jug of water he refuses to drink
bags of fluid draining into a good site
pastel stripes separating cancer patients

I expect the ringing of bells
but there are only those sounds outside
my hearing
his body's quiet implosion
time

> *I'm just going to lie back and sleep a little bit*
> *Do you want me to go Dad?*
> *No stay   just stay*

fingers of women/marking time

desire

1.

song knowing   somnambulant
desire   sleep and dream
un/speakable
song throated   space filling

2.

suck sugar
soundless and melt   sweet
in your mouth
taste   melts sweet
in mine

3.

to you   *je t'aime*
I give sounds strange
                throat songs
pass to you
                words round
                        smooth
a stone on my tongue

rope

loosened sheets
laze against our
night pressing bodies

slit between the blind
lightacrossanklesbed
white rope joins us
binds flesh and
bone against bone
wrist and pulse
night knotted

day undoes us
the rope fades
fast as
sunrise: 7:12

train trestle

fingers
skinny
over the dirt road's
rib curve

in
tall weeds
we've outrun our shadows
mimic lines of track
quiet before the train

comes shaking past the two of us
murmur of grass
summer warmed

touch sites

sensing parts
printed with the match of
your lines
on fingerpads palm of hand

lip search
over skin tongue seeking
lips
snake and taste
mouth over mind
mouth over body
what matters
is earlobes small globes
chin and lidded eyes

sensing parts
made visible
sites of touch
blades kneecaps
jumble of bones
threaded by muscle
skin covering construction

fingers of women/marking time

push salon-curled hair
under scarves
chiffon and bright
hide in
matching gloves

fasten buttons
on camel coats
smell of lotion
powder
soap

snap shut
compartments of wallets
search for bills
coppers
silver

save pennies
pay the waitress
at Woolworth's luncheonette
drum the table
when service is slow

scrape peas from
splayed pods
laying open
seagreenpeagreen
like hulls of wrecked ships

scrubbed clean
with soap
before cooking
supper/pick
at the bones

fidget twitch
tap in time to
the weight and rhythm
of the song
they are thinking

don't talk
with their hands
clasped in their laps
grips locked
fingers silenced

waitress suite

1.

her feet
        soaked in a big speckled blue roaster
        filled with warm water and Epsom salts

like a ballet dancer's
            sore   misshapen
            nubs on the small curled fifth toes hard red
            follow her everywhere
                        haunt every step

she would cut both those toes right off
        but she would only have to
        clean up the mess afterward

2.

bones
scrimshaw story   this day's dance

from milkshake machine
                its long chrome snout poking
                milk and real ice cream

from coffee cup
            to coffeepot
            cream and sugar
            salt and pepper

3.

white shoes and stockings
      one-piece uniform   two pockets on top
                                two on the bottom   deep
her order pad and pencil
coding customers' desires
frz cffe blt
      black ink ciphers
          on white paper

she is invisible
          except to open eyes of grease
          floating solemnly on top
          soup of the day

4.

list of things to make:

> do
> over
> up
> extra work for yourself
> extra work for myself
> the best of it
> your bed and lie in it

5.

her white waitress shoes
swollen sore bruised
beaten by hard tile floor

she slipped out of them
at the end of the day
death masks
knobs of bone
recorded in scuffed white leather

6.

head anchored
in a chairback
thin rind of her eyes stretched closed

       only her feet move
       in a saltwater dance

7.

waitress

at the Regal Bowl   five- and ten-pin bowling

had to transfer buses twice
her daughter asked how much would she be making   she
said she didn't know
she hadn't wanted to ask   just glad to have a job
period

in the Depression she worked as a
hired girl
got 20 bucks plus room and board
for a winter's work

in the spring she spent two
on a pair of shoes
from the Eaton's catalogue
they came COD

she wore them only to dance
Saturday night
drawing slender black leather straps
to music made by his fiddle's bow

now he accused her of getting into strange cars
taking rides from strange men

8.

scrub brush

its rhythm travelling across old lino
up her arm across her shoulders
her neck
insinuating its sound into her
mouth

      keep mouth shut head down

when they were still on the farm
she had cleared scrub brush
so she could plant her garden
pulled nameless bushes
jutting grass   fibril roots
held their deaths   strings
bunched in her bare hands
      the front paw of their barn cat ripped away
      strings of sinew
      the cat had licked   slowly
      oblivious to what she had lost

elements of expectation

hand-washed white sheets
hung out to dry
shake themselves over
the soil black beds
in the stone-walled garden
sown patchy

inside
a rose in water opens

five spoons full
from a tin
tea boiled loose and black
smelling like strawberries

black currant jam
from a jar
spread sparingly
touching the outline
of a thin slice
of bread

a pinch
from a jar of salt
crystal white and elemental
sprinkled scratchy on an egg
soft-boiled with the top
cracked off

spooning out still-steaming yolk
scooping away the inside
from the brown shell
skin white at the point of power

movement of fingers and knuckles
obvious little bones
small links
between thought and action

noise

water drips into a bowl
where frozen meat thaws
its noise
screams through the house

smell of muddy boots
in the porch
weeds in the garden
beginning to show
empty milk bottles
shivering against a cold concrete step
distractions
to keep yourself from silence

wash day

in a dug-out dirt basement
a wringer washer and two metal tubs
one to rinse   one to carry

        even in winter
        clothes pinned on the line
        steam leaving their bodies   spirits
        rising into cold   disappearing

towels brought back in   twisted
smelling of frost and hard as tree bark

        my mother's hands   red
        laid out
        shirts   socks   pants
        on the kitchen table

the frozen shapes we wore
their cold shells
melting on my skin

my mother's relationship with fire

1.   glued to cardboard
        burnt matches
        shape of a cross

2.   beside the gas stove
        tin repository
        wooden snakes
        bright red heads

3.   roughness on the side of the box
        smell of sulphur
        so pretty   so peaceful
        eating   the wood
        to her fingertips
        lighting one   after   another
        hidden in the bedroom
        flames   licked   curtains
        glowing   tongues
        quiet   watching

        I had my fingers burnt
        to cure me
        but it didn't work
        we got garter snakes
        oodles of them
        from the bush
        threw them in a tub
        rubbery and squirming
        hit them with a stick
        poured gas on them and
        set them on fire

4.   photo
my mother and father
at sixteen
outside a gas station
making funny faces
my father wearing someone's
cat's-eye glasses
laughing
gathering wood
dry grass and sticks
adding paper to the pile
watching the fire catch
in the middle of the highway
on the black road   black night

5.   her wedding dress
white lace stiff-skirted
for years
stored in a closet
filling a green garbage bag
saved from suffocation
she made a fire
stuffed the dress between paper and kindling
poked at the covered buttons down
the back   billowing skirt
lace filaments glowing

Jean

my grandmother covered herself
with variegated afghans and tried
to cover me with:

> *don't cut your nose off*
> *to spite your face*

which turned out
to be good advice because
she also told me to

> *stop and smell the roses*

knitting

needles click
furrowed rows of stitches
saffron-coloured wool
skein diminishes
a casting off
as unconscious
as breathing
as children's
connected lives unlocked/unravelled
in another country

        saffron is precious
        separation of stigma/petal
        pistil of the purple crocus
        dissolves in water
        colours what it touches
        is absorbed
        something foreign in an Irish

house   plants and towels
in her tub
bits of soap worn smooth
slivers of stone
amethyst brooch
tea and biscuits
eats like a bird   skeleton
key in the lock
a prayer for those who live alone
a prayer to St. Anthony for something
lost

conversations:
her books
Marguerite de Valois
The Life of Charlotte Brontë
halo around the open door
narrow band of light

saffron colours
rice pudding
the colour of church candle flames
the colour of the yolk inside
an egg
sacred mysteries
martyrs   blessed bones
pilgrimage of a precious spice

needles cross/click
a stitch is cast off
as the rosary
rhythm of prayer

company

clock said midnight
the fridge shuddered whirred weary
time perishable by degrees

her legs up on a shabby blanket
covered chair
late movie smell of empty bottles
stacked in the porch
coats on hooks and nails
their missing buttons in a glass jar
on a window ledge with his razor

he is back
and brings company
until the bottle's gone

she goes to bed by herself
door closed listening
to a late-night radio phone-in show
something she's picked up

ghosts

1.

people coming home
late at night
had seen the road light up
ghost of a woman cross
silent birds fly
motionless trees glow silver

skeptics said
        it's only the reflection
        of headlights
but after a fire
went through that bush
she was never seen again

2.

a secondwind well after midnight
scrubbing floors
screeching
outside the door
a fighting cock?

she checked the house
to see that everyone
still slept
climbed in beside her husband
smell of scrub water
still on her hands

3.

femme phantasm
perfume smell at 2 a.m.
grapes of wraith
cold corners
spider crawl nails
spirit hands
catch things that
fall from walls
eager to help
shady voyeurs
women you
can't get rid of

she

is a woman candled in a doorway
holding open   her door
holding shut her sweater

is a woman neither in nor out
waiting on the threshold
for an opening

is a woman who washes roughly
thoroughly inspects
                          surfaces

is a woman who listens
for sounds between
tines of forks   teeth of combs

is a woman writing on the quiet
hiding words between mattress and boxspring
pages of books   teeth   and   tongue

secret language

dolphin-shaped frost
plunges on glass   cold
from the outside in
       flings itself through Highlands in
       between Ada Boulevard
               and 118th Avenue
shabby in the shadow
of the archdiocese
and the smell of Gainers
       when the wind blows
       the wrong way

I teach this dolphin
tricks
           dive and arc
on my window stuck
tongue on frozen metal
pinned   happy captive

       I am learning its language
       its secret language
       on frost riding air

words about birth

fine lines on a peacock's feather
now a tracery of bone curving on screen
and beating heart

> wake and spread your fingers
> open your fist and let me
> look at what you hold

W<small>ENDY</small> M<small>C</small>G<small>RATH</small>'s poetry has been published in *CV2, Prism international, NeWest Review, Tessera, Room of One's Own, Orbis,* and *Grain.* Her verse has been broadcast on CBC Radio and her work has appeared in several anthologies. Previously she published *Go Van Gogh,* a chapbook of her poetry. In 1998 she received the James Patrick Folinsbee Prize from the University of Alberta's Department of English. She lives in Edmonton, Alberta, with her husband and two sons.